****
LITTLE
BOOK OF
JEWISH
FEASTS
****

LITTLE
BOOK
OF
JEWISH

* *

FEASTS

* *

LEAH KOENIG

Photographs by **LINDA PUGLIESE**

CHRONICLE BOOKS
SAN FRANCISCO

The Little Book series is a collection of thematic Jewish cookbooks that will be published serially. Each book will include a bite-size collection of meticulously curated and category-defining global Jewish recipes. Packaged in slim, gorgeously designed books, a single volume—or the whole series—will fit perfectly on and enhance an already overcrowded bookshelf.

Text copyright © 2018 by Leah Koenig.
Photographs copyright © 2018 by Chronicle Books LLC.
All rights reserved. No part of this book may be reproduced
in any form without written permission from the publisher.
Library of Congress Cataloging-in-Publication Data available.
ISBN: 978-1-4521- 6062-7
Manufactured in China

Designed by Vanessa Dina
Photographs by Linda Pugliese
Food styling by Monica Pierini
Prop styling by Paige Hicks
Typesetting by Frank Brayton

10 9 8 7 6 5 4 3 2

Chronicle Books LLC
680 Second Street
San Francisco, California 94107
www.chroniclebooks.com

To Carol and Rena, makers of feasts.

Jewish tradition has two houses of worship. The first, of course, is the synagogue, where Jewish communities have joined in prayer and contemplation for generations. The second is the Shabbat and holiday table. It is there, over braided loaves of challah and the bubbling cacophony of laughter and conversation, that memories are made. It is there that families gather and reconnect and heirloom recipes are brought forth to the table like offerings of love and devotion. It is there that traditions are passed down— not through formal instruction, but through the sensory pleasures that come with eating together.

It is no accident that the table has taken on a primary role in Jewish life. When the Holy Temple in Jerusalem was destroyed nearly two thousand years ago, the head rabbis of the era actively shifted many of the central aspects of temple worship and ritual to the home.

The table became the symbolic stand-in for the altar—the place where blessings over wine and bread were said and where candles were lit in place of the glowing menorah that once sat at the heart of the Holy Temple. Meals became much more than just a collection of dishes— they were sacred manifestations of Jewish practice.

It is not surprising, then, that nearly every Jewish holiday has a large meal (or several!) associated with it. On Passover, a feast is sandwiched in between the seder's four cups of wine. On Purim day, families sit down for a large, festive meal. On Sukkot, meals are eaten outside in a temporary dwelling structure known as a sukkah. (For more on the holidays and their traditions, see page 111.) At each holiday, the family around the table, and naturally the food on it, are paramount.

In America, Jewish holiday meals have become synonymous with roast chicken and juicy brisket. The collection of beloved holiday main dishes in this book includes inspired versions of those Ashkenazi classics—a roast chicken (page 75) flavored with aromatic leeks, tender parsnips, and briny Meyer lemon, and a sweet-tangy brisket (page 99) braised with balsamic vinegar and brown sugar. But it also delves into Sephardi and Mizrahi cuisines to offer celebratory Jewish dishes from across the globe. For Rosh Hashanah, there's the Persian chicken, walnut, and pomegranate stew called Fesenjan (page 81) and an intricately spiced Seven-Vegetable Tagine (page 41) from Morocco. For Hanukkah, there's crunchy-crusted fried chicken (page 83), which Italian Jews favor over Eastern Europe's potato latkes. And on Passover, there's Mina (page 35)—a savory matzo pie with leeks and spinach that Sephardi Jews enjoy.

No matter if it's the first time or the hundredth, hosting a Shabbat or holiday meal can be intimidating. In addition to hoping the food tastes good, there are thousands of years and layers upon layers of tradition to uphold and renew. But with family and friends around the table, raising glasses, singing together, and passing serving platters around, all the stress and the prep become worthwhile. This cookbook offers a collection of showstopping main dishes that will delight everyone at the table, including the cook!

CHAPTER 1

VEGETARIAN AND FISH DISHES

Jewish holiday cooking is traditionally associated with meat—and lots of it. But there are plenty of celebratory vegan, vegetarian, and pescatarian dishes to enjoy, especially on holidays like Shavuot, Hanukkah, and Yom Kippur, when dairy meals are more common. From egg- and cheese-laden soufflés and butter-crusted savory pies to hearty bean and vegetable stews, this section brings meat-free mains to the center of the table.

Eggplant Kuku (Persian Frittata)

SERVES 6

This Persian take on a frittata is packed with bites of creamy sautéed eggplant and a bundle of fresh, green herbs. A kuku is rarely out of place on an Iranian-Jewish table. It is usually served as part of the mezze spread or as a side dish, but it is hearty enough to stand alone as a main course, particularly at vegetarian meals. It can often be found at a festive Purim meal, in commemoration of the biblical story of Esther, which took place in ancient Persia. And thanks to the generous amount of oil that goes into a kuku, it is also a favorite dish for Hanukkah celebrations.

⅓ CUP [80 ML] VEGETABLE OIL, PLUS MORE FOR THE PAN

2 MEDIUM ONIONS, HALVED THROUGH THE ROOT AND THINLY SLICED

KOSHER SALT AND FRESHLY GROUND BLACK PEPPER

1 SMALL EGGPLANT (ABOUT 1 LB [455 G]), PEELED AND CUT INTO ½-IN [12-MM] PIECES

7 EGGS

2 TBSP ALL-PURPOSE FLOUR

1 TSP BAKING POWDER

½ CUP [25 G] FINELY CHOPPED FRESH FLAT-LEAF PARSLEY

2 TBSP CHOPPED FRESH OREGANO

4 GARLIC CLOVES, MINCED OR PUSHED THROUGH A PRESS

1 TSP GROUND TURMERIC

1 TSP ONION POWDER

¼ TSP RED PEPPER FLAKES

3 OZ [85 G] FETA, FINELY CRUMBLED (OPTIONAL)

continued

1. Preheat the oven to 375°F [190°C] and brush a 9-in [23-cm] springform or regular round cake pan with oil. Line the pan with parchment paper (use scissors to cut out a circle of parchment for the bottom and a long strip to wrap around the sides), then brush the parchment lightly with oil.

2. Heat the 1/3 cup [80 ml] oil in a large sauté pan over medium heat. Add the onions, season with a little salt, and cook, stirring occasionally, until soft and lightly browned, 8 to 10 minutes. Add the eggplant and continue cooking, stirring occasionally, until softened and lightly browned, about 10 minutes. Remove from the heat and let cool slightly.

3. Meanwhile, whisk together the eggs, flour, baking powder, parsley, oregano, garlic, turmeric, onion powder, red pepper flakes, 3/4 tsp salt, and a generous amount of pepper in a large bowl. Gently fold in the eggplant mixture and feta (if using). Pour into the prepared pan.

4. Bake until golden brown and cooked through, 35 to 40 minutes. Remove from the oven and set aside on a wire rack to cool for 15 minutes. Gently remove from the pan, peel off the parchment, and slice into wedges or squares. Serve warm or at room temperature. Store leftovers, covered, in the fridge for up to 3 days.

Kousa b'Jibn
(Crustless Zucchini Quiche)

SERVES 4 TO 6

A jibn is the Syrian equivalent of a crustless quiche—a mix of cheese, eggs, and vegetables that gets baked until beautifully browned and savory. *Jibn* is Arabic for cheese, and the dish often includes a couple of different types. In this case, sharp Cheddar is joined by cottage cheese, which amplifies its richness and flavor. Jibn is a wonderful make-ahead dish that reheats well and is delicious warm or at room temperature, which is likely why so many Syrian Jewish families include them on their Yom Kippur breakfast table. It would also be a lovely, cross-cultural dish for families that follow the Ashkenazi custom of eating dairy foods on Shavuot. To speed up the prep time, shred the zucchini and Cheddar in a food processor fitted with a shredding blade.

2 TBSP VEGETABLE OIL, PLUS MORE FOR BRUSHING

1 MEDIUM ONION, FINELY CHOPPED

KOSHER SALT AND FRESHLY GROUND BLACK PEPPER

2 LB [910 G] ZUCCHINI (ABOUT 4 MEDIUM), PEELED AND GRATED ON THE LARGE HOLES OF A BOX GRATER

6 EGGS, LIGHTLY BEATEN

1½ CUPS [120 G] GRATED SHARP CHEDDAR CHEESE

1½ CUPS [360 G] COTTAGE CHEESE

½ TSP ONION POWDER

continued

1. Preheat the oven to 350°F [180°C] and brush a 9-in [23-cm] square baking pan with about 1 tsp of oil. Line the pan with parchment paper, then brush the parchment lightly with oil.

2. Heat the 2 Tbsp oil in a large skillet set over medium heat. Add the onion and a pinch of salt and cook, stirring occasionally, until soft and translucent, 5 to 7 minutes. Turn the heat to medium-high, add the zucchini, and cook until nearly all the liquid has evaporated, 20 to 25 minutes. Remove from the heat and let cool slightly.

3. Meanwhile, combine the eggs, Cheddar cheese, cottage cheese, onion powder, 1/2 tsp salt, and 1/2 tsp pepper in a large bowl and mix well. Gently fold in the cooked zucchini mixture. Pour into the prepared baking pan.

4. Bake until lightly browned and cooked through, 40 to 50 minutes. Remove from the oven and set on a wire rack to cool. Cut into squares and serve warm or at room temperature. Store leftovers, covered, in the fridge for up to 2 days.

Blintz Soufflé

SERVES 8 TO 10

Ashkenazi Jews have a custom of serving dairy foods on the holiday of Shavuot. Aside from cheesecake, blintzes filled with soft cheese and fried in butter are perhaps the most iconically indulgent dish. Typically, blintzes are fried and served individually. But some home cooks have adapted the recipe to feed a crowd, layering the filled rolls into a casserole dish and covering them with a sweet, eggy custard. The soufflé emerges from the oven puffed and golden, the perfect dairy centerpiece for a festive Shavuot lunch or Yom Kippur break-fast meal. Blintz soufflé is a great make-ahead dish, as it can be assembled the night before serving, covered, and refrigerated (unbaked) overnight. In the morning, preheat the oven and bake as directed. And while nothing tops the flavor or sense of culinary accomplishment that comes with making this dish entirely from scratch, frozen cheese blintzes can be substituted for the homemade. Thaw approximately 18 blintzes enough to separate them, then arrange snugly in the baking dish, and top with the egg custard.

BLINTZ WRAPPERS

1½ CUPS [360 ML] MILK

5 EGGS

¼ CUP [50 G] SUGAR

2 CUPS [280 G] ALL-PURPOSE FLOUR

1 TSP VANILLA EXTRACT

½ TSP KOSHER SALT

UNSALTED BUTTER FOR FRYING (ABOUT 6 TBSP [85 G])

continued

2 CUPS [480 G] RICOTTA CHEESE
4 OZ [115 G] CREAM CHEESE, AT ROOM TEMPERATURE
2 TBSP SUGAR
½ TSP GROUND CINNAMON

CUSTARD

2 TBSP UNSALTED BUTTER, MELTED
5 EGGS, LIGHTLY BEATEN
1½ CUPS [360 G] SOUR CREAM
½ CUP [100 G] SUGAR
½ TSP FINELY GRATED ORANGE ZEST
¼ CUP [60 ML] ORANGE JUICE
1 TSP VANILLA EXTRACT
¼ TSP GROUND CINNAMON
¼ TSP KOSHER SALT

FRESH RASPBERRIES OR SLICED STRAWBERRIES FOR SERVING

1. Make the blintz batter: Combine the milk, eggs, sugar, flour, vanilla, and salt in a food processor and process, scraping down the sides of the bowl as necessary, until smooth. It should be the consistency of heavy cream. Let the batter rest at room temperature for at least 30 minutes to allow the gluten to relax.

2. Meanwhile, make the filling: Stir together the ricotta, cream cheese, sugar, and cinnamon in a small bowl until combined; cover and refrigerate until ready to use.

3. Tear or cut out 18 squares of parchment paper and set aside. (These will go between the blintz wrappers as you cook and stack them—no need to cut them precisely.) Melt approximately 1 tsp of butter in an 8-in [20-cm] nonstick skillet set over medium heat. Once hot, pour 1/4 cup [60 ml] of the batter into the pan; immediately pick up the pan and swirl it in all directions to coat the bottom evenly with a thin layer of batter. Cook until the bottom is golden and the center is just dry, about 1 minute. (Do not flip the blintz wrapper.) Remove the wrapper with a spatula and place it on a piece of parchment paper. Continue making the wrappers, adding more butter to the pan as needed and stacking the wrappers in between the sheets of parchment as you go. You should end up with about 18 wrappers.

4. Fill the wrappers: Spoon 2 heaping Tbsp of the filling onto the lower third of each wrapper, leaving 1/2 in [12 mm] at the bottom uncovered. Fold that 1/2 in [12 mm] up over the filling, then fold in each side toward the center. Roll the blintz up and away from you, tucking the filling inside in a neat package. Lay the filled blintz, seam-side down, on a plate and continue assembling blintzes with the remaining wrappers and filling.

5. Make the custard and assemble the soufflé: Preheat the oven to 350°F [180°C]. Brush the bottom of a 9-by-13-in [23-by-33-cm] baking dish with the melted butter. Arrange the filled blintzes, seam-side down, in the bottom of the

continued

dish. If necessary, squeeze them together a little to fit. In a large bowl, whisk together the eggs, sour cream, sugar, orange zest, orange juice, vanilla, cinnamon, and salt. Pour the custard mixture over the blintzes.

6. Bake until puffed and golden brown, 40 to 50 minutes. Remove from the oven and let cool on a wire rack for 10 to 15 minutes. Serve warm, topped with berries. Store leftovers, covered, in the fridge for up to 3 days.

Berkuks (Sweet Couscous with Milk)

SERVES 6

American cooks typically regard couscous as a side dish. But according to Ron and Leetal Arazi of New York Shuk—an artisanal company that makes harissa and other Middle Eastern pantry staples—Moroccan Jews consider it a main event on Purim. Berkuks can be served savory or sweet. The key to both variations is the generous amount of butter and decadent splash of milk stirred into the still-warm couscous. Any good-quality butter works well for this recipe, but if you can find cultured butter, which has a deeper and more complex flavor, it is worth trying. To warm the milk, heat the desired amount in a small saucepan set over medium heat until just warmed through.

2½ CUPS [600 ML] WATER

½ TSP KOSHER SALT

2 CUPS [360 G] DRIED COUSCOUS

4 TBSP [55 G] UNSALTED BUTTER, AT ROOM TEMPERATURE

¼ CUP [50 G] SUGAR

1 TSP GROUND CINNAMON, PLUS MORE FOR SERVING

SLICED ALMONDS, SLIVERED DATES, AND SLIVERED DRIED APRICOTS FOR SERVING

WHOLE MILK, WARMED, FOR SERVING

1. Stir the water and salt together in a medium saucepan set over high heat; bring to a boil. Pour the couscous into the boiling water in a steady stream, stirring constantly. Remove the pan from the heat, cover the saucepan, and let stand for 10 minutes. Fluff with a fork.

continued

2. Meanwhile, stir together the butter, sugar, and cinnamon in a medium bowl until combined. Add to the still-warm cooked couscous and fold to incorporate. Mound the couscous onto a serving platter and decorate as desired with almonds, dates, apricots, and an additional sprinkle of cinnamon. Serve with warmed milk on the side, to pour into individual bowls at the table. Store leftovers, covered, in the fridge, for up to 2 days.

Hortopita (Wild Greens Pie)

SERVES 8 TO 10

Like their neighbors, Greek Jews foraged for greens in the spring and incorporated them into their home cooking. That includes hortopita (literally, greens pie), a double-crusted pastry stuffed with any number of wild greens, as well as fragrant fresh herbs and briny cheese. Hortopita's verdant color and bright flavor taste like an edible celebration of springtime, making it the perfect centerpiece for the Shavuot table. The dough encasing this version is sturdier than the paper-thin filo traditionally used, but lends a solid, buttery base that pairs well with the tender filling. For the tastiest results, slice the kale as thinly as possible using the following method: Remove the woody stems and stack the leaves on top of one another in a pile. Starting at the bottom, tightly roll up the stack like a jelly roll. Using a sharp knife, slice perpendicular to the roll to create thin ribbons.

DOUGH

3½ CUPS [490 G] ALL-PURPOSE FLOUR, PLUS MORE FOR DUSTING

½ TSP KOSHER SALT

1 CUP [220 G] COLD UNSALTED BUTTER, CUT INTO SMALL PIECES

2 EGGS

¼ CUP [60 ML] COLD WATER, OR MORE AS NEEDED

FILLING

2 TBSP EXTRA-VIRGIN OLIVE OIL, PLUS MORE FOR THE BAKING DISH

3 MEDIUM LEEKS, WHITE AND LIGHT GREEN PARTS, THINLY SLICED

KOSHER SALT

1 SMALL BUNCH KALE, STEMMED AND THINLY SLICED

continued

4 EGGS

½ TSP ONION POWDER

1 TSP DRIED OREGANO

8 OZ [230 G] FETA, FINELY CRUMBLED

4 OZ [115 G] PECORINO OR PARMESAN CHEESE, GRATED

½ TSP FRESHLY GROUND BLACK PEPPER

5 OZ [140 G] BABY ARUGULA OR BABY SPINACH

1 CUP [50 G] CHOPPED FRESH DILL

½ CUP [25 G] CHOPPED FRESH FLAT-LEAF PARSLEY

1. Make the dough: Combine the flour, salt, and butter pieces in a large food processor and pulse until the butter is incorporated and the flour has a crumbly appearance, like cornmeal. Add the eggs and pulse to incorporate, scraping down the sides of the bowl as necessary. With the motor running, drizzle in the water and process until the dough forms into a soft and pliable, but not sticky, ball. If necessary, drizzle in more water, 1 tsp at a time, until the desired consistency is reached. Gather the dough and divide it into two equal pieces. Pat each piece into a disk, cover with plastic wrap, and let rest in the fridge for at least 1 hour, or up to 2 days.

2. Make the pie: Preheat the oven to 350°F [180°C] and lightly grease a 9-by-13-in [23-by-33 cm] baking dish with a little olive oil. Heat the 2 Tbsp olive oil in a large sauté pan set over medium heat. Add the leeks and a pinch of salt and cook, stirring occasionally, until softened, about 10 minutes. Add the kale, cover the pan, and cook, stirring occasionally, until slightly wilted, about 5 minutes. Remove from the heat and let cool to the touch.

3. Beat together 3 of the eggs, the onion powder, and oregano in a very large bowl. Stir in the feta, pecorino, 1 tsp of salt, and the pepper. Add the cooked leeks and kale (discarding any excess liquid from cooking), the arugula, dill, and parsley, and, using your hands, mix until the greens are evenly coated with the egg and cheese mixture.

4. Lightly flour a large flat surface and roll out one of the disks of dough into a large, very thin rectangle. If the dough is too firm to roll out, let it rest at room temperature for 5 minutes and try again. Drape the dough over the prepared baking dish and arrange so that it fully covers the bottom and sides. Transfer the greens mixture to the baking dish and spread into an even layer. Roll out the second piece of dough in the same manner and drape over the top. Trim the dough that hangs over the edges, leaving about 1 in [2.5 cm], then crimp the sides. Cut several thin slits into the top of the dough with a sharp knife.

5. Beat the remaining egg with 1 tsp water in a small bowl and brush the egg wash over the top of the pie. (You will not use all of the egg wash.) Bake until golden brown, 35 to 45 minutes. Remove from the oven and let stand for at least 30 minutes before slicing into squares. (The greens continue to steam and soften as the pie cools.) Serve warm or at room temperature. Store leftovers, covered, in the fridge for up to 5 days.

Mina (Matzo Pie with Leeks and Spinach)

SERVES 8

From bourekas to pastelito (miniature pies), many Sephardi Jewish communities maintain a deep affection for savory pastries. But on Passover, the options for baking are limited by the weeklong prohibition of chametz—foods made from wheat, rye, barley, spelt, or oats. Enter mina, a free-form pie that is typically layered with spiced meat and vegetables or, as it is here, with spinach and feta cheese. Brightened with lemon zest and a burst of fresh oregano, this take on mina has all the briny fresh flavor of a boureka. Serve it as the main dish for a vegetarian or pescatarian seder meal, or at any dinner throughout the holiday.

3 TBSP UNSALTED BUTTER, PLUS MORE FOR THE BAKING DISH

3 LARGE LEEKS, WHITE AND LIGHT GREEN PARTS, THINLY SLICED

2 MEDIUM SHALLOTS, FINELY CHOPPED

KOSHER SALT AND FRESHLY GROUND BLACK PEPPER

5 OZ [140 G] BABY SPINACH

4 GARLIC CLOVES, FINELY CHOPPED

1 TBSP FINELY CHOPPED FRESH OREGANO LEAVES

4 CUPS [960 G] COTTAGE CHEESE

4 EGGS

¼ CUP [60 ML] MILK

1 CUP [140 G] CRUMBLED FETA

½ TSP FINELY GRATED LEMON ZEST

9 SHEETS MATZO

FINELY CHOPPED FRESH FLAT-LEAF PARSLEY FOR SERVING

continued

1. Melt the butter in a large skillet set over medium heat. Add the leeks, shallots, and a pinch of salt and cook, stirring occasionally, until softened, about 10 minutes. Add the spinach, garlic, and oregano and continue cooking until the spinach wilts, 2 to 3 minutes. Remove from the heat and let cool slightly.

2. Whisk together the cottage cheese, 3 of the eggs, the milk, feta, lemon zest, 1/2 tsp salt, and a generous amount of pepper in a medium bowl.

3. Preheat the oven to 350°F [180°C] and rub a little butter around the bottom and sides of a 9-by-13-in [23-by-33-cm] baking dish. Fill a second shallow baking dish with warm water and dip in 3 sheets of matzo. Let the matzo soften for 2 to 3 minutes. Shake off the excess water and arrange the matzo sheets in the bottom of the prepared baking dish. Break the third matzo, if necessary, to fit it into the dish. Cover with approximately half of the cheese mixture, followed by half of the leek and spinach mixture. Repeat the process with 3 more softened matzo sheets and the remaining cheese and spinach mixtures.

4. Soften the remaining 3 sheets of matzo and arrange on the top. Whisk the remaining egg in a small bowl and brush generously over the top of the matzo.

5. Bake until golden brown and bubbling, about 45 minutes. Remove from the oven and let stand for 10 minutes. Serve warm, sprinkled with parsley. Store leftovers, covered, in the fridge for up to 4 days.

Mushroom Moussaka

SERVES 8 TO 10

Greek Jews are no strangers to moussaka—the rich casserole traditionally made from eggplant and lamb and thickly layered with béchamel. But because kosher laws prohibit the consumption of milk and meat together, Jewish versions of the dish tend to either skip the béchamel entirely, which is a shame, flavorwise, or make a dairy-free topping from fat, flour, and stock. In this take, the moussaka's eggplant base is paired with cremini mushrooms instead of lamb, making it completely meat-free and perfectly suited for its creamy topping. Moussaka is warming, hearty, and easily transportable, making it the perfect dish for alfresco meals on Sukkot.

BASE AND SAUCE

¼ CUP [60 ML] EXTRA-VIRGIN OLIVE OIL, PLUS ABOUT ¾ CUP [180 ML] FOR GREASING AND BRUSHING

4 SMALL EGGPLANTS (ABOUT 1 LB [455 G] EACH), PEELED

KOSHER SALT AND FRESHLY GROUND BLACK PEPPER

2 MEDIUM ONIONS, FINELY CHOPPED

1 LB [455 G] CREMINI MUSHROOMS, STEMMED AND CUT INTO ½-IN [12-MM] PIECES

6 GARLIC CLOVES, MINCED OR PUSHED THROUGH A PRESS

1 TBSP DRIED OREGANO

1 TSP GROUND CINNAMON

¼ TSP GROUND ALLSPICE

ONE 28-OZ [800-G] CAN CRUSHED TOMATOES

BÉCHAMEL

6 TBSP [85 G] UNSALTED BUTTER

½ CUP [70 G] ALL-PURPOSE FLOUR

continued

3 CUPS [720 ML] MILK

1 CUP [30 G] FINELY GRATED PARMESAN CHEESE

KOSHER SALT AND FRESHLY GROUND BLACK PEPPER

3 EGG YOLKS

1. Make the base and sauce: Preheat the oven to 400°F [200°C] and generously grease two large rimmed baking sheets with about 3 Tbsp of olive oil each. Slice 3 of the eggplants into 1/2-in- [12-mm-] thick rounds. Arrange the eggplant slices in a single layer on the sheets, brush the tops generously with more oil, and season with salt and pepper. Bake, flipping the eggplant pieces once, until softened and lightly browned, 20 to 25 minutes. Remove from the oven and set aside. Lower the oven temperature to 350°F [180°C].

2. Meanwhile, chop the remaining eggplant into 1/2-in [12-mm] cubes. Heat the 1/4 cup [60 ml] of oil in a large sauté pan set over medium heat. Add the onions and a pinch of salt and cook, stirring occasionally, until soft and translucent, 5 to 7 minutes. Add the chopped eggplant and mushrooms, turn the heat to medium-high, and cook, stirring occasionally, until the vegetables are very tender and the liquid has cooked off, 10 to 15 minutes. Stir in the garlic, oregano, cinnamon, and allspice and cook until fragrant, about 1 minute. Stir in the crushed tomatoes, 1 tsp salt, and 1/2 tsp pepper. Turn the heat to medium and simmer until slightly thickened, 5 to 10 minutes. Taste and add more salt and pepper, if desired.

continued

3. Make the béchamel: Melt the butter in a medium sauce-pan set over medium heat. Add the flour and whisk until fully combined, then slowly whisk in the milk. Simmer, whisking constantly, until the sauce thickens enough to coat the back of a spoon, 5 to 10 minutes. Whisk in about half of the Parmesan, 1 tsp salt, and a generous amount of pepper. In a separate small bowl, whisk the egg yolks until smooth. Whisking constantly, slowly drizzle about 1/2 cup [120 ml] of the hot béchamel into the yolks. Turn the heat under the saucepan to medium-low and slowly whisk the tempered egg mixture back into the béchamel. Remove from the heat.

4. Assemble the moussaka: Grease the bottom of a 9-by-13-in [23-by-33-cm] baking dish. Layer half of the eggplant slices in the bottom of the baking dish and cover with half of the sauce. Layer the remaining eggplant slices into the dish and cover with the remaining sauce. Evenly pour the béchamel over the top, smoothing with a rubber spatula. Sprinkle with the remaining Parmesan.

5. Bake until bubbling and golden brown on top, 20 to 25 minutes. Remove from the oven and let stand for 15 minutes before serving. Serve hot. Store leftovers, covered, in the fridge for up to 3 days.

Seven-Vegetable Tagine

SERVES 6 TO 8

Moroccan Jews serve this spiced tagine on Rosh Hashanah. The seven distinct vegetables (which vary from cook to cook) are said to represent the Jewish calendar's seventh month, Tishrei, which is the month when Rosh Hashanah falls. They also signify the abundant bounty of the fall harvest season. The addition of raisins to the dish adds a delightful sweetness, while the chickpeas transform it into a complete vegetarian meal. Serve the tagine over steamed couscous, which soaks up the delicious stew. To streamline the preparation process, measure out all the spices before you start cooking and add them in all at once.

¼ CUP [30 G] SLICED ALMONDS

¼ CUP [60 ML] EXTRA-VIRGIN OLIVE OIL

2 MEDIUM ONIONS, HALVED THROUGH THE ROOT
AND THINLY SLICED

4 PLUM TOMATOES (ABOUT 1 LB [455G]), SEEDED AND CHOPPED

2 GARLIC CLOVES, FINELY CHOPPED

1 TSP GROUND CINNAMON

1 TSP SWEET PAPRIKA

1 TSP GROUND GINGER

½ TSP GROUND TURMERIC

½ TSP GROUND CUMIN

½ TSP GROUND CORIANDER

½ TSP RED PEPPER FLAKES

ONE 15-OZ [430-G] CAN CHICKPEAS, RINSED AND DRAINED

2 ZUCCHINI, HALVED LENGTHWISE AND SLICED INTO
½-IN [12-MM] HALF-MOONS

continued

2 CUPS [280 G] PEELED AND FINELY CHOPPED BUTTERNUT SQUASH

**2 LARGE CARROTS, PEELED, HALVED LENGTHWISE,
AND CUT INTO ½-IN [12-MM] PIECES**

⅓ CUP [45 G] GOLDEN RAISINS

2½ CUPS [600 ML] VEGETABLE STOCK

KOSHER SALT AND FRESHLY GROUND BLACK PEPPER

CHOPPED FRESH FLAT-LEAF PARSLEY FOR GARNISH

1. Put the almonds in a large pan set over medium-low heat and toast, shaking the pan occasionally, until fragrant and lightly browned, 5 to 7 minutes. Remove the pan from the heat and let cool; set aside.

2. Heat the oil in a medium saucepan set over medium-high heat. Add the onions and cook, stirring occasionally, until softened and lightly browned, 7 to 10 minutes. Add the tomatoes and cook, stirring occasionally, until softened, 3 to 5 minutes. Add the garlic, cinnamon, paprika, ginger, turmeric, cumin, coriander, and red pepper flakes and cook, stirring, until fragrant, 1 to 2 minutes.

3. Add the chickpeas, zucchini, butternut squash, carrots, raisins, stock, 1 tsp salt, and a generous amount of pepper and bring the mixture to a simmer. Turn the heat to low, cover the pot, and cook until the squash and carrots are tender, about 20 minutes. Uncover and continue cooking, stirring occasionally, until the sauce thickens slightly, about 10 minutes. It will still be somewhat liquidy, but should more closely resemble a stew than a soup. Taste and add more salt, if desired. Serve hot, sprinkled with parsley and almonds. Store leftovers, covered, in the fridge for up to 5 days.

Loubia (Black–Eyed Pea Stew)

SERVES 8

Egyptian and Syrian Jews traditionally serve black-eyed peas (*loubia* in Arabic) on Rosh Hashanah, with the peas symbolizing fertility and success in the New Year. Black-eyed peas are ready to harvest in the early fall in the Middle East, which also makes them seasonally appropriate for the holiday. Loubia can be prepared with meat, usually lamb or veal, and is typically offered as a side. But served alongside bread and a salad, these spicy stewed beans make a hearty and nourishing vegetarian main dish. This version swaps half of the black-eyed peas for creamy white beans, giving the final dish an added layer of texture. Prep note: Grate the tomatoes on the large holes of a box grater set over a large bowl to capture all of the pulp and juice. Or use a food processor fitted with a shredding blade.

1 CUP [180 G] DRIED BLACK-EYED PEAS

1 CUP [160 G] DRIED WHITE BEANS (SUCH AS CANNELLINI)

¼ CUP [60 ML] EXTRA-VIRGIN OLIVE OIL, PLUS MORE FOR DRIZZLING

2 MEDIUM ONIONS, FINELY CHOPPED

2 MEDIUM CARROTS, PEELED AND FINELY CHOPPED

6 GARLIC CLOVES, FINELY CHOPPED

KOSHER SALT AND FRESHLY GROUND BLACK PEPPER

1 TSP GROUND CUMIN

1 TSP ONION POWDER

1 TSP SUGAR

1 TSP SMOKED PAPRIKA

½ TSP GROUND GINGER

½ TSP CAYENNE PEPPER

continued

4 LARGE TOMATOES (ABOUT 1½ LB [680 G]), GRATED
2 TBSP TOMATO PASTE
3 CUPS [720 ML] VEGETABLE STOCK, PLUS MORE AS NEEDED
CHOPPED FRESH CILANTRO OR FLAT-LEAF PARSLEY FOR SERVING

1. Combine the black-eyed peas and white beans in a large bowl and add enough water to cover by about 2 in [5 cm]. Cover the bowl with a dish towel, soak the beans overnight, and then drain, rinse, and drain again.

2. Heat the olive oil in a large saucepan set over medium heat. Add the onions, carrots, garlic, and a generous pinch of salt and cook, stirring occasionally, until the vegetables begin to soften, 8 to 10 minutes. Add the cumin, onion powder, sugar, paprika, ginger, and cayenne and cook, stirring, until fragrant, 1 to 2 minutes.

3. Stir in the grated tomato pulp and the tomato paste. Bring to a simmer and cook, stirring occasionally, until the mixture thickens slightly, about 10 minutes. Add the drained beans, the stock, 2 tsp salt, and 1/2 tsp black pepper; raise the heat to medium-high and bring the mixture to a simmer. Turn the heat to medium-low and cook, partially covered and stirring occasionally, until the beans are tender and creamy, 1 to 1 1/2 hours. If the pot begins to look dry during cooking, add more stock, 1/2 cup at a time. Taste and add more salt and pepper, if desired.

4. Remove the pan from the heat and let stand for about 10 minutes. Serve hot or warm, drizzled with more olive oil and sprinkled with cilantro. Store leftovers, covered, in the fridge for up to 3 days.

Fennel and Mustard Seed Gravlax

SERVES 8

For Ashkenazi Jews, a Yom Kippur break-fast meal isn't complete without a platter of cured fish and a heap of bagels to go with it. Making gravlax—a Nordic preparation of raw salmon that gets cured with salt, sugar, and dill—takes a bit of advance planning, but is a simple and mostly hands-off culinary project. This version spikes the dry cure with fragrant fennel seeds, mustard seeds, and lemon zest. Sliced thin and draped over a bagel with cream cheese, it is a perfect, make-ahead showstopper for the holiday break-fast table—or any brunch gathering.

2 TBSP BLACK PEPPERCORNS

1 TBSP FENNEL SEEDS

1 TBSP MUSTARD SEEDS

⅔ CUP [110 G] KOSHER SALT

½ CUP [100 G] PACKED LIGHT BROWN SUGAR

ZEST OF 2 LEMONS

1½ TO 2 LB [680 TO 910 G] SKIN-ON SALMON FILLET, RINSED AND THOROUGHLY PATTED DRY

1½ CUPS [75 G] FINELY CHOPPED FRESH DILL

1. Combine the peppercorns, fennel seeds, and mustard seeds in a small sauté pan set over medium heat and toast, shaking the pan occasionally, until they begin to pop, 1 to 2 minutes. Transfer to a plate to cool, then add to a mortar and pestle and coarsely crush. In a large bowl, mix together the crushed spices, the salt, brown sugar, and lemon zest.

continued

2. Stretch a layer of plastic wrap into a shallow baking dish large enough to hold the salmon, letting the plastic wrap hang over the edges of the dish by several inches. Sprinkle with half of the salt mixture. Using a sharp knife, make a few shallow cuts on the skin side of the salmon and place it on top of the salt mixture, flesh-side up. Cover with the remaining salt mixture and 1 cup [50 g] of the dill.

3. Fold the ends of the plastic wrap around the salmon and cover snugly with additional plastic wrap. Refrigerate the salmon for 48 to 72 hours, turning the package once a day and using your fingers to redistribute the brine. Drain off any liquid that accumulates in the dish. When ready, the salmon should feel firm to the touch at the thickest part.

4. Unwrap the salmon and rinse the fillet well under water, discarding the spices and brine in the baking dish; pat dry. Spread the remaining 1/2 cup [25 g] dill on a plate. Firmly press the flesh side of the salmon into the dill to coat it, brushing off any excess dill with your fingers. Use a sharp knife to thinly slice the gravlax against the grain. Serve cold. Store leftovers, covered, in the fridge for up to 3 days.

Roasted Salmon with Lemon–Dill Sauce

SERVES 6 TO 8

While it may seem counterintuitive to modern sensibilities, the kosher prohibition against serving meat and dairy together does not extend to fish. As a result, fish dishes are regularly served as the main course at milchig (dairy) meals. In America, poached or roasted salmon topped with a creamy dill sauce has become a popular entrée for such meals, sometimes on Shabbat and particularly on Shavuot, when dairy foods are highlighted. In this version, the zesty green sauce is brightened with lemon zest and juice and sharpened with chopped shallot.

VEGETABLE OIL FOR GREASING AND BRUSHING

8 SKIN-ON SALMON FILLETS (ABOUT 6 OZ [170 G] EACH), PATTED DRY

KOSHER SALT AND FRESHLY GROUND BLACK PEPPER

1 CUP [240 G] MAYONNAISE

⅓ CUP [80 G] SOUR CREAM

½ TSP FINELY GRATED LEMON ZEST

2 TBSP FRESH LEMON JUICE

½ CUP [25 G] PACKED FRESH DILL (STEMS OKAY), PLUS MORE CHOPPED DILL FOR GARNISH

2 TBSP FINELY CHOPPED SHALLOT

¼ TSP ONION POWDER

¼ TSP GARLIC POWDER

continued

1. Preheat the oven to 400°F [200°C] and grease two baking dishes. Rub or brush the salmon fillets on both sides with a little vegetable oil, then season both sides with salt and pepper. Place them, skin-side down, onto the prepared baking dishes. Roast until the salmon is pale pink and cooked through, about 10 minutes (longer for thicker pieces of fish). Remove from the oven and let cool slightly.

2. Meanwhile, combine the mayonnaise, sour cream, lemon zest, lemon juice, dill, shallot, onion powder, garlic powder, 1/4 tsp salt, and 1/4 tsp pepper in a food processor and process, scraping down the sides of the bowl as necessary, until smooth. Taste and add more salt, if desired.

3. Transfer the fillets to a serving platter. Serve warm or at room temperature, sprinkled with a little more dill and with the lemon-dill sauce on the side for drizzling. Store leftovers, covered, in the fridge for up to 2 days.

Chraime (Spicy Sephardi Fish Fillets)

SERVES 4

Stemming from an Arabic word meaning hot, chraime is a fragrant stewed fish dish that gets its dose of heat from minced chiles, or, in this version, dried red pepper flakes. North African Jews enjoy chraime for Shabbat dinner and also serve it on Rosh Hashanah and at the Passover seder. Like many Jewish fish dishes, chraime is typically eaten as a prelude to the main course, but it easily holds its own at the center of the table. This take on chraime keeps the fiery spice to a minimum, but to dial up the heat, add more red pepper flakes to taste. Serve chraime with Israeli couscous or rice.

¼ CUP [60 ML] VEGETABLE OIL

1 LARGE ONION, FINELY CHOPPED

6 GARLIC CLOVES, PEELED AND THINLY SLICED

½ TSP GROUND CUMIN

½ TSP GROUND CINNAMON

½ TSP GROUND TURMERIC

½ TSP SWEET PAPRIKA

½ TSP RED PEPPER FLAKES, OR MORE TO TASTE

ONE 14½-OZ [415-G] CAN DICED TOMATOES

½ CUP [120 ML] WATER

3 TBSP TOMATO PASTE

1 TBSP MINCED PRESERVED LEMON PEEL

1 TSP SUGAR

1 BAY LEAF

1½ TSP KOSHER SALT

½ TSP FRESHLY GROUND BLACK PEPPER

continued

**4 SKINLESS HALIBUT OR RED SNAPPER FILLETS
(ABOUT 6 OZ [170 G] EACH), RINSED AND PATTED DRY**

**CHOPPED FRESH CILANTRO OR FLAT-LEAF PARSLEY
FOR SERVING**

LEMON WEDGES FOR SERVING

1. Heat the oil in a large wide pan set over medium heat. Add the onion and cook, stirring occasionally, until softened, 6 to 8 minutes. Add the garlic, cumin, cinnamon, turmeric, paprika, and red pepper flakes and cook, stirring, until fragrant, 1 to 2 minutes. Stir in the diced tomatoes, water, tomato paste, preserved lemon peel, sugar, bay leaf, salt, and pepper. Raise the heat slightly and bring the mixture to a boil. Turn the heat to medium-low and nestle the fish fillets in the sauce, spooning the sauce over the top of the fillets to cover, if necessary. Cover the pan and simmer until the fish is cooked through, about 20 minutes.

2. Using a flat spatula, carefully remove the fillets from the pan and transfer to a serving platter. Let the remaining sauce continue to cook in the pan, stirring often, until it thickens slightly, about 5 minutes. Remove the pan from the heat, discard the bay leaf, and spoon the sauce over the fish. Serve sprinkled with cilantro and with the lemon wedges on the side. Store leftovers, covered, in the fridge for up to 2 days.

Pesce All'Ebraica
(Sweet and Sour Jewish Fish)

SERVES 6

Italian Jewish cuisine boasts many wonderful fish recipes, including this one. Traditionally served on Rosh Hashanah or the meal before Yom Kippur, as well as on Shabbat, it provides a festive feel and ample flavor without a lot of effort. Pesce All'Ebraica is traditionally flavored with pine nuts and raisins—ingredients that attest to the great influence Arabic cooking (introduced to Jews in Sicily and other parts of Southern Italy by traders) had on Jewish cuisine. This version maintains the pine nuts but substitutes the raisins with plump red grapes, which have a juicier bite.

½ CUP [60 G] PINE NUTS

⅓ CUP [80 ML] EXTRA-VIRGIN OLIVE OIL

⅓ CUP [80 ML] RED WINE VINEGAR

3 TBSP MILD HONEY

1¼ TSP KOSHER SALT, PLUS MORE FOR SPRINKLING

6 LARGE SHALLOTS, HALVED AND THINLY SLICED

6 GARLIC CLOVES, PEELED AND THINLY SLICED

1½ CUPS [240 G] SEEDLESS RED GRAPES, HALVED

6 MEDIUM FIRM FISH FILLETS (SUCH AS SOLE OR FLOUNDER; ABOUT 2 LB [910 G] TOTAL)

¼ TSP FRESHLY GROUND BLACK PEPPER

continued

1. Preheat the oven to 400°F [200°C]. Put the pine nuts in a small sauté pan set over medium-low heat and toast, shaking the pan occasionally, until fragrant and lightly browned, about 5 minutes. Remove the pan from the heat and let cool.

2. Whisk together the olive oil, roasted pine nuts, vinegar, honey, and the 1/4 tsp salt until well combined in a medium bowl. Arrange the shallots, garlic, and grapes on the bottom of a 9-by-13-in [23-by-33-cm] baking dish. Drizzle about half of the oil and vinegar mixture over the top. Lay the fillets in a single layer on top of the shallots and grapes (slightly overlapping is okay), sprinkle with a little more salt and the pepper, and drizzle with the remaining oil and vinegar mixture.

3. Cover the baking dish with aluminum foil and bake for 10 minutes. Uncover and continue baking, basting occasionally with the pan juices, until the fish is tender and cooked through, 10 to 20 minutes. Serve hot or at room temperature, with pan juices, roasted shallots, and grapes spooned over the fish. Store leftovers, covered, in the fridge for up to 2 days.

SETTING THE JEWISH HOLIDAY TABLE

The holidays offer the perfect excuse to get festive with decorations. Here are a few tips that will add beauty to any holiday table.

EMBRACE COLOR

The traditional Jewish holiday table in America tends to utilize a lot of white and silver—white tablecloth and white napkins alongside silver candlesticks, silver kiddush cups, silverware, and so on. The effect is elegant, but can look a bit formal. For a more free-spirited look, mix things up by spreading the table with a colorful tablecloth or tapestry, or top a white linen cloth with colorful napkins and dishes. Using mismatched vintage plates with different complementary patterns gives the table a look that is at once homey and stylish.

GET CREATIVE

Holidays are sacred, but they do not need to be stuffy—there are plenty of ways to add personality to the table! Try incorporating holiday symbols into the decor. Scatter gold and silver foil–wrapped gelt and small wooden dreidels on the table for Hanukkah. For a Purim meal, make simple DIY place cards by setting a gragger (the noisemaker used while reading the story of Queen Esther) inscribed with guests' names at each plate. And on Passover, delight younger (and young-at-heart) guests by arranging ten plagues–inspired figurines across the tabletop.

HIGHLIGHT THE SEASON

The Jewish calendar is cyclical, with holidays arriving during the same season every year, so play up that seasonality at the table. Incorporate fruits and plants (like pomegranates on Rosh Hashanah, gourds and dried corn on Sukkot, stalks of wheat on Shavuot, or potted fresh parsley for Passover) into the centerpieces. And be sure to use seasonal flowers.

BRING OUT THE HEIRLOOMS

Did you inherit silverware, special dishes, or other tableware from family members? Holidays are the perfect time to enjoy them. It connects the meal to the generations that came before and brings memories of loved ones to the table.

CHAPTER 2

CHICKEN, BEEF, AND LAMB DISHES

Jewish families across the globe pull out all the stops for holiday meals, laying out a feast for family and friends. Historically, even families with little means did whatever they could to ensure they had special meat dishes at the Shabbat table. This section focuses on the deeply comforting main dishes—saucy braised chicken, long-simmered brisket, savory lamb stew, and crackling fried schnitzel— that taste like home for the holidays.

Chicken with Quince and Almonds

SERVES 6

Related to apples and pears, quinces come into season in autumn, and they are a hallmark of High Holiday meals across Sephardi and Mizrahi cuisines. They possess an intoxicating floral fragrance, a starchy, potato-like texture, and, when braised, a gentle flavor that pairs wonderfully with braised chicken. In this version, a splash of apple cider vinegar and a drizzle of honey gives the dish a bright sweetness that would stand out on the Rosh Hashanah table. Look for quinces in season at specialty produce markets and farmers' markets. The fruit's center can be quite tough, so take care to remove the entire core and all the seeds (using the same method you would to core an apple) before cooking.

½ CUP [60 G] SLICED ALMONDS

3 LARGE QUINCES, PEELED, CORED,
AND SLICED INTO ½-IN [12-MM] WEDGES

4 LB [1.8 KG] SKIN-ON CHICKEN THIGHS AND LEGS, PATTED DRY

KOSHER SALT AND FRESHLY GROUND BLACK PEPPER

2 TBSP VEGETABLE OIL, PLUS MORE AS NEEDED

1 LARGE ONION, HALVED THROUGH THE ROOT AND THINLY SLICED

1 TSP GROUND CINNAMON

1 CUP [240 ML] CHICKEN STOCK

¼ CUP [60 ML] APPLE CIDER VINEGAR

2 TBSP HONEY

½ TSP SAFFRON THREADS, CRUSHED

CHOPPED FRESH FLAT-LEAF PARSLEY FOR SERVING

continued

1. Put the almonds in a small sauté pan set over medium-low heat and toast, shaking the pan occasionally, until fragrant and lightly browned, about 5 minutes. Remove the pan from the heat and let cool; set aside.

2. Layer the quince wedges on the bottom of a large casserole dish; set aside. (The quince will turn brown as it oxidizes—that is okay.) Sprinkle the chicken pieces on both sides with salt and pepper. Heat the 2 Tbsp vegetable oil in a large sauté pan set over medium-high heat. Working in batches, brown the chicken pieces, starting skin-side down and flipping once, until browned on both sides, 8 to 10 minutes per batch. If the bottom of the pan begins to look dry, add a little more oil, as needed. Layer the browned chicken pieces on top of the quince.

3. Preheat the oven to 375°F [190°C], then make the braising liquid: Set the same sauté pan you used to brown the chicken over medium heat. Add the onion and a pinch of salt and pepper and cook, stirring occasionally, until browned, 6 to 8 minutes. Stir in the cinnamon and cook for 1 minute.

4. Whisk together the stock, vinegar, honey, saffron, and 1/2 tsp salt in a medium bowl. Add the mixture to the pan, scraping up any browned bits from the bottom of the pan. Turn the heat to high, bring to a boil, then carefully pour the braising liquid over the chicken and quinces. Cover the dish with aluminum foil and cook in the oven until the chicken is fork-tender, 50 to 55 minutes. Remove from the heat and let rest.

5. Meanwhile, transfer 1 1/2 cups [360 ml] of the braising liquid to a saucepan set over high heat, and bring to a boil. Cook, stirring often, until the liquid reduces by two-thirds, 10 to 15 minutes. Spoon the reduced sauce over the chicken and sprinkle with toasted almonds and parsley. Serve hot. Store leftovers, covered, in the fridge for up to 3 days.

Chicken Fricassee

SERVES 6

Chicken fricassee is Ashkenazi soul food at its finest—savory, hearty, and a comforting shade of brown. Jewish home cooks originally took to the dish as a way of transforming the odds and ends of a chicken (gizzards, necks, wings, feet, and so on) into a flavorful stew that could feed a crowd. In America, cooks began to add small meatballs to the mix as a way of stretching the dish even further. Over time, chicken fricassee has fallen out of fashion, but it remains perfectly at home on the Shabbat, Rosh Hashanah, or (when made with potato starch and matzo meal) Passover table. This version takes contemporary tastes into consideration, using a mix of chicken wings and legs and adding a splash of white wine and aromatic bay leaf to the gravy. Serve the chicken and meatballs over egg noodles, matzo farfel, or rice, with plenty of challah, rye bread, or matzo alongside to sop everything up.

2 TBSP VEGETABLE OIL, PLUS MORE AS NEEDED

3 LB [1.4 KG] SKIN-ON CHICKEN WINGS AND LEGS, PATTED DRY

KOSHER SALT AND FRESHLY GROUND BLACK PEPPER

2 MEDIUM ONIONS, HALVED THROUGH THE ROOT AND THINLY SLICED

2 STALKS CELERY, FINELY CHOPPED

2 MEDIUM CARROTS, PEELED AND FINELY CHOPPED

6 GARLIC CLOVES, THINLY SLICED

⅓ CUP [45 G] ALL-PURPOSE FLOUR, OR ⅓ CUP [60 G] POTATO STARCH

½ CUP [120 ML] DRY WHITE WINE

3 CUPS [720 ML] CHICKEN STOCK

continued

1 BAY LEAF

1 TBSP SWEET PAPRIKA

8 OZ [230 G] GROUND BEEF

¼ CUP [35 G] UNSEASONED DRIED BREAD CRUMBS OR MATZO MEAL

½ TSP ONION POWDER

1 EGG, LIGHTLY BEATEN

1. Heat the 2 Tbsp oil in a large Dutch oven or other large, heavy saucepan with a lid set over medium-high heat. Season the chicken with salt and pepper. Working in batches, brown the chicken pieces, turning once, until browned on both sides, 8 to 10 minutes per batch. If the bottom of the pan begins to look dry, add a little more oil, as needed. Transfer the browned chicken pieces to a bowl and set aside.

2. Lower the heat to medium, add the onions, celery, carrots, and garlic to the pan and cook, stirring occasionally, until softened and lightly browned, 6 to 8 minutes. Add the flour and stir to coat the vegetables, then stir in the white wine, scraping up any browned bits from the bottom of the pan, and cook until the liquid evaporates, about 2 minutes. Add the chicken stock, bay leaf, paprika, 1 tsp salt, and ½ tsp pepper, raise the heat to medium-high, and bring to a boil.

3. Add the browned chicken pieces (it is okay if the liquid doesn't cover them all the way). Lower the heat to low, cover, and cook, stirring occasionally, until the chicken is tender, about 1 hour. The mixture should bubble along at a slow, steady simmer. If it isn't bubbling enough, nudge the heat up. If it's bubbling too furiously, nudge it down.

4. Meanwhile, make the meatballs: Mix together the ground beef, bread crumbs, onion powder, egg, and 1/4 tsp salt in a large bowl. Scoop out the mixture by the level Tbsp and form into 1/2-in [12-mm] meatballs. After the chicken has cooked for an hour, add the meatballs, raise the heat to medium, and continue cooking, covered, until cooked through, 15 minutes. Remove from the heat and let stand for 10 to 15 minutes before serving. Serve hot. Store leftovers, covered, in the fridge for up to 3 days.

Roast Chicken with Leek, Meyer Lemon, and Parsnip

SERVES 4

A roast chicken is perhaps the most iconic centerpiece of the Ashkenazi holiday table—and for good reason. A majestically browned bird and a waft of savory perfume as it hits the table are the things Shabbat, Rosh Hashanah, and Passover memories are made of. Potatoes and carrots are commonly found underneath a roast chicken, but I prefer a mix of sweet parsnips and aromatic leeks, which soften and caramelize in the oven. Along with copious cloves of garlic, they capture and absorb the chicken's drippings, soaking up an unbelievable amount of flavor. The Meyer lemon, meanwhile, is mellower than a regular lemon, and imparts a gentle tang to the dish. If they are unavailable, a standard lemon makes a fine substitute.

5 MEDIUM PARSNIPS, PEELED, HALVED LENGTHWISE, AND CUT INTO 1-IN [2.5-CM] CHUNKS

3 MEDIUM LEEKS, WHITE AND LIGHT GREEN PARTS, HALVED LENGTHWISE AND CUT INTO 1-IN [2.5-CM] CHUNKS

2 HEADS GARLIC, CLOVES SEPARATED AND PEELED

1 MEYER LEMON, THINLY SLICED

10 SPRIGS FRESH THYME

4 TBSP [60 ML] EXTRA-VIRGIN OLIVE OIL

KOSHER SALT AND FRESHLY GROUND BLACK PEPPER

4 LB [1.8 KG] SKIN-ON CHICKEN THIGHS AND LEGS, PATTED DRY

continued

1. Preheat the oven to 475°F [240°C]. Scatter the parsnips, leeks, garlic cloves, lemon slices, and thyme sprigs in the bottom of a large roasting pan or baking dish. Drizzle the vegetables with 2 Tbsp of the olive oil and sprinkle generously with salt and pepper; toss until the vegetables are evenly coated with oil.

2. Lay the chicken pieces on top of the vegetables. Drizzle the remaining 2 Tbsp of olive oil evenly on the chicken, rubbing it in to coat both sides, then sprinkle with salt and pepper. Arrange a few of the thyme sprigs on top of the chicken pieces.

3. Roast for 25 minutes. Turn the oven temperature to 400°F [200°C], baste the chicken with pan juices, then continue cooking until the skin is browned, the juices run clear, and a thermometer stuck into the thickest part of a thigh reaches 165°F [75°C], 25 to 30 minutes longer. Remove from the oven and let rest for 10 to 15 minutes before serving. Serve hot. Store leftovers, covered, in the fridge for up to 3 days.

Sofrito (Braised Chicken with Fried Potatoes)

SERVES 6 TO 8

Sofrito refers to dishes (commonly chicken or veal) that are browned and then slowly cooked, resulting in a richly savory dish. In this version, the chicken is braised in stock that has been flavored with paprika, turmeric, and cardamom until it is falling off the bone. Near the end of cooking, fried potatoes are added and simmered just long enough to let the crisp skin soak in the sauce. Sofrito is a beloved staple of Sephardi Shabbat dinners and also commonly served as a warming main dish on Sukkot. Serve it with rice and challah or pita for mopping up the remaining sauce.

3 TBSP VEGETABLE OIL, OR MORE AS NEEDED

4 LB [1.8 KG] SKIN-ON CHICKEN THIGHS AND LEGS, PATTED DRY

KOSHER SALT AND FRESHLY GROUND BLACK PEPPER

4 MEDIUM YUKON GOLD POTATOES (1½ LB [680 G]), PEELED AND CUT INTO 2-IN [5-CM] PIECES

1 LARGE ONION, HALVED THROUGH THE ROOT AND THINLY SLICED

2 TSP SWEET PAPRIKA

1 TSP GROUND TURMERIC

¼ TSP GROUND CARDAMOM

½ TSP ONION POWDER

½ TSP GARLIC POWDER

1½ CUPS [360 ML] CHICKEN STOCK

1 BAY LEAF

continued

1. Heat the 3 Tbsp oil in a large Dutch oven or other large heavy saucepan with a lid set over medium-high heat. Season the chicken with salt and pepper. Working in batches, brown the chicken pieces, turning once, until browned on both sides, 8 to 10 minutes per batch. Transfer the browned chicken pieces to a large plate and set aside.

2. If the bottom of the pan looks dry, add 1 Tbsp of oil. Working in two batches, add the potato pieces to the pan and cook, stirring occasionally, until browned and crisp all over, about 10 minutes per batch. The potatoes will not be fully softened at this point. Transfer the fried potatoes to a bowl and set aside.

3. Add the onion and a sprinkle of salt and stir. Cover the pan, turn the heat to medium, and cook, stirring occasionally, until the onion is softened and browned, 8 to 10 minutes. Stir in the paprika, turmeric, cardamom, onion powder, garlic powder, 1/2 tsp salt, and 1/4 tsp pepper and cook until fragrant, about 1 minute.

4. Add the browned chicken pieces, the stock, and the bay leaf, cover, turn the heat to medium-low, and cook, stirring occasionally, until the chicken is tender, 40 to 50 minutes. Add the potatoes and gently stir to submerge them in the cooking liquid. Raise the heat to medium and cook, uncovered, until the cooking liquid has thickened slightly and the potatoes are fully tender, about 10 minutes. Taste and add more salt or pepper, if desired. Remove the bay leaf and serve hot. Store leftovers, covered, in the fridge for up to 3 days.

Fesenjan (Persian Chicken, Walnut, and Pomegranate Stew)

SERVES 6 TO 8

This saucy stew, which is thickened with finely ground walnuts, is beloved throughout Iran. Traditionally it was made with duck, but, over time, chicken has become a common substitute. Persian Jews often serve the dish on Rosh Hashanah or autumnal Shabbats, when pomegranates are at their seasonal peak. It gets sweetened with pomegranate molasses, a thick syrup made from boiled pomegranate juice that is available online and at specialty food markets. Sprinkled with fresh, ruby-colored pomegranate seeds and bright green parsley, it sits handsomely at the center of the meal. Serve fesenjan with lots of rice to catch all the flavorful sauce.

2½ CUPS [300 G] WALNUT HALVES

3 TBSP VEGETABLE OIL

2½ LB [1.2 KG] BONELESS, SKINLESS CHICKEN THIGHS, CUT INTO 2-IN [5-CM] PIECES

KOSHER SALT AND FRESHLY GROUND BLACK PEPPER

1 LARGE ONION, FINELY CHOPPED

2 CUPS [480 ML] CHICKEN STOCK

1 BAY LEAF

1 CUP [240 ML] POMEGRANATE MOLASSES

2 TBSP HONEY, OR MORE AS NEEDED

½ TSP GROUND TURMERIC

½ TSP GROUND CINNAMON

POMEGRANATE SEEDS FOR SERVING

CHOPPED FRESH FLAT-LEAF PARSLEY FOR SERVING

continued

1. Put the walnuts in a large pan set over medium-low heat and toast, shaking the pan occasionally, until fragrant and lightly browned, 5 to 7 minutes. Remove the pan from the heat and let cool. Transfer the cooled nuts to a food processor and pulse until finely ground with a few slightly larger pieces. Set aside.

2. Meanwhile, heat 2 Tbsp of the oil in a Dutch oven or other large wide saucepan set over medium-high heat. Season the chicken pieces on both sides with salt and pepper. Working in batches, sear the chicken pieces, turning once, until golden on both sides, 2 to 3 minutes per side. Transfer the seared chicken pieces to a plate and set aside.

3. Add the remaining 1 Tbsp of oil to the Dutch oven along with the onion and a pinch of salt. Cook, stirring occasionally, until softened and lightly browned, 6 to 8 minutes. Stir in the ground walnuts, chicken stock, bay leaf, pomegranate molasses, honey, turmeric, cinnamon, 1 tsp salt, and 1/4 tsp pepper. Bring the mixture to a boil, then turn the heat to medium-low, add the browned chicken pieces back to the pan, cover, and cook, stirring often, until the chicken is cooked through, about 30 minutes. Uncover the pan, turn the heat to medium, and continue cooking, stirring often, until the sauce thickens into a rich stew, 10 to 15 minutes.

4. Remove from the heat, taste, and stir in a little more salt, pepper, or honey, if desired. Serve hot with pomegranate seeds and parsley sprinkled over the top. Store leftovers, covered, in the fridge for up to 3 days.

Pollo Fritto per Hanukkah
(Fried Chicken for Hanukkah)

SERVES 4 TO 6

Hanukkah commemorates the story of the Maccabees, a small Judean army that recaptured the Temple in Jerusalem from the ancient Greeks. According to the story, the Maccabees were able to find only enough oil to light the Temple's menorah for one night, but the oil miraculously lasted for eight days. In honor of that "miracle of oil," Jewish communities celebrate Hanukkah by eating all manner of fried foods. Potato latkes and jelly doughnuts called sufganiyot are the most widely known of these dishes in America. But in Italy, the focus is decidedly on *pollo fritto—* crunchy, oil-kissed fried chicken. This version of *pollo fritto* quick-marinates the chicken pieces with a mix of lemon, garlic, cinnamon, and thyme for an added dimension of flavor. Serve the fried chicken with extra lemon wedges for squeezing or with your favorite dipping sauce.

4 LB [1.8KG] SKIN-ON CHICKEN THIGHS AND LEGS, PATTED DRY

ZEST AND JUICE FROM 2 LEMONS (ABOUT ¼ CUP [60ML] JUICE)

3 GARLIC CLOVES, MINCED OR PUSHED THROUGH A PRESS

1 TSP KOSHER SALT, PLUS MORE FOR SPRINKLING

½ TSP FRESHLY GROUND BLACK PEPPER

½ TSP GROUND CINNAMON

1 TSP DRIED THYME

VEGETABLE OIL FOR FRYING

1½ CUPS [210 G] ALL-PURPOSE FLOUR

2 TSP ONION POWDER

2 TSP GARLIC POWDER

4 EGGS

continued

1. Combine the chicken, lemon zest and juice, garlic, 1 tsp salt, pepper, cinnamon, and thyme in a large bowl with a tight-fitting lid. Cover the bowl and shake to coat the chicken. Refrigerate for at least 1 and up to 2 hours (not longer, or the meat will be tough once cooked).

2. Fill a Dutch oven or large deep cast-iron pan with 1 1/2 in [4 cm] of oil and set over medium heat until the oil reaches 375°F [190°C] on an instant-read thermometer. Meanwhile, line a large plate with several layers of paper towels and set aside. Stir together the flour, onion powder, and garlic powder in a wide shallow bowl. Beat the eggs in another bowl.

3. Remove the chicken pieces from the marinade and brush off any garlic or lemon zest. Dredge the chicken pieces in the flour mixture on both sides, shaking off the excess. Dip in the egg to coat, allowing the excess to drip off, then dip once more in the flour. Working in batches, if necessary, add the coated chicken pieces to the hot oil and fry, turning occasionally, until the chicken is golden brown and cooked through, 15 to 20 minutes per batch. An instant-read thermometer stuck into the deepest part of a thigh should read 165°F [75°C]. If frying in batches, add additional oil to the pan as necessary. Transfer the fried chicken to the prepared plate to drain and sprinkle with a little more salt. Serve immediately. Store leftovers, covered, in the fridge for up to 3 days.

Poppy Seed Schnitzel

SERVES 6 TO 8

Along with falafel, sabich, and shawarma, chicken schnitzel
is one of Israel's most popular street foods. It is also commonly made by home cooks, as it's a simple, satisfying main
dish that can feed a crowd. The basic recipe of chicken
cutlets dredged in egg and bread crumbs can be dressed
up in countless ways, and on Purim, some families add
poppy seeds to the mix in honor of the holiday's connection
to *mohn* (Yiddish for poppy seed). In this version, they are
joined by sesame seeds, giving the breading a delightful
crunch and nutty flavor. Serve the cutlets with a squeeze
of lemon, mayonnaise mixed with harissa, or your favorite
flavorful dip.

1 CUP [140 G] ALL-PURPOSE FLOUR

2 TSP ONION POWDER

2 TSP GARLIC POWDER

1 TSP SWEET PAPRIKA

4 EGGS

1 CUP [60 G] PANKO BREAD CRUMBS

½ CUP [70 G] SESAME SEEDS

¼ CUP [35 G] POPPY SEEDS

6 BONELESS, SKINLESS CHICKEN BREASTS

KOSHER SALT AND FRESHLY GROUND BLACK PEPPER

VEGETABLE OIL FOR FRYING

LEMON WEDGES FOR SERVING

continued

1. Stir together the flour, onion powder, garlic powder, and paprika in a wide shallow bowl or small baking dish. Beat the eggs in another bowl. Stir together the bread crumbs, sesame seeds, and poppy seeds in a third bowl.

2. Using a sharp knife, carefully butterfly each chicken breast, then use a meat mallet to gently pound each piece to a 1/4 in [6 mm] thickness. You should end up with 12 relatively uniform pieces of chicken breast. Season the chicken pieces on both sides with salt and pepper. Dredge the chicken pieces in the flour mixture on both sides, shaking off the excess. Dip in the egg to coat, allowing the excess to drip off, then coat well with the seeded bread crumbs.

3. Heat 1/4 in [6 mm] of vegetable oil in a large skillet set over medium-high heat. Line a large plate with several layers of paper towels. Working in batches, add the coated chicken pieces to the hot pan and cook, turning once, until crispy and cooked through, 5 to 6 minutes total. Transfer the chicken to the prepared plate to drain. Serve hot with lemon wedges on the side for squeezing. Store leftovers, covered, in the fridge for up to 2 days. To reheat, arrange in a single layer on a rimmed baking sheet and heat in a 400°F [200°C] oven until warmed through, about 10 minutes.

T'fina Pakaila
(White Bean and Meatball Stew)

SERVES 6 TO 8

This savory stew is a highlight of the Tunisian table on Shabbat and is also served during Rosh Hashanah and Sukkot. The base is made from a combination of meaty flanken, creamy white beans, and spinach. Some families add a traditional North African sausage called *osbane*, while others sub in delicately spiced meatballs. Like many stews, T'fina Pakaila tastes even better the second day, which makes it a wonderful make-ahead main dish.

MEATBALLS

1 LB [455 G] GROUND BEEF

1 SMALL ONION, GRATED, WITH ITS LIQUID RESERVED

¼ CUP [35 G] UNSEASONED DRIED BREAD CRUMBS

1 TBSP GROUND CUMIN

1 TSP GROUND CINNAMON

1 TSP SMOKED PAPRIKA

½ TSP GROUND CORIANDER

½ TSP ONION POWDER

2 TSP KOSHER SALT

½ TSP FRESHLY GROUND BLACK PEPPER

2 EGGS, LIGHTLY BEATEN

2 TBSP EXTRA-VIRGIN OLIVE OIL

STEW

¼ CUP [60 ML] EXTRA-VIRGIN OLIVE OIL

1 LB [455 G] BEEF FLANKEN OR SHORT RIBS

KOSHER SALT AND FRESHLY GROUND BLACK PEPPER

1 LARGE ONION, FINELY CHOPPED

continued

6 GARLIC CLOVES, CHOPPED

5 CUPS [1.2 L] BEEF OR CHICKEN STOCK

ONE 15-OZ [430-G] CAN WHITE BEANS, RINSED AND DRAINED

5 OZ [140 G] BABY SPINACH

¼ CUP [10 G] FINELY CHOPPED FRESH MINT

HARISSA FOR SERVING

1. Make the meatballs: Combine the ground beef, grated onion with its liquid, bread crumbs, cumin, cinnamon, paprika, coriander, onion powder, salt, pepper, and eggs in a large bowl and mix with your hands to combine. Form the meat mixture into tightly rolled 1-in [2.5-cm] balls and set aside. You should end up with about 35 meatballs.

2. Heat the 2 Tbsp olive oil in a large saucepan set over medium-high heat. Working in batches, add the meatballs and cook, turning, until browned on all sides, about 4 minutes per batch. Transfer the browned meatballs to a large plate and refrigerate until needed.

3. Make the stew: Scrape up any debris from the bottom of the saucepan the meatballs were cooked in and wipe it clean. Pour the ¼ cup [60 ml] olive oil into the saucepan and set over medium-high heat. Season the flanken with salt and pepper and cook, turning, until browned on all sides, 6 to 8 minutes total. Transfer the browned ribs to a plate. Add the onion and garlic to the saucepan and cook, stirring, until softened, 6 to 8 minutes. Return the ribs to

continued

the saucepan, add the stock, and bring to a boil. Turn the heat to medium-low, cover, and cook until the flanken is tender, about 1 hour.

4. Add the meatballs and white beans, turn the heat to medium, and simmer, uncovered, until the meatballs are cooked through, 8 to 10 minutes. Stir in the spinach and mint and cook until the spinach wilts, about 2 minutes. Taste and add more salt and pepper, if desired. Serve hot, swirled with harissa to taste. Store leftovers, covered, in the fridge for up to 3 days.

Holishkes (Stuffed Cabbage)

SERVES 8 TO 10

Stuffed vegetables are ubiquitous across Jewish cuisine. On a practical level, they help stretch expensive ingredients, like meat, to feed a family. On a symbolic level, stuffed foods are commonly served on Sukkot, when the themes of harvest and abundance are at the forefront. In Ashkenazi cuisine, stuffed cabbage served in a sweet and sour sauce is likely the best-known (and best-loved) filled vegetable. In twentieth-century America, some cooks began to add a can of jellied cranberry sauce to the tomato base. While it may seem unusual, the cranberries lent a welcome tang and color to the dish. And since cranberries are indigenous to North America, it was a nice (if unintended) way to help the European dish settle into its new surroundings. This version of the recipe nods to these home cooks' ingenuity, incorporating fresh or frozen whole cranberries instead of the canned variety.

1 LARGE HEAD GREEN CABBAGE (ABOUT 4 LB [1.8 KG])

½ CUP [100 G] LONG-GRAIN WHITE RICE

1½ CUPS [160 G] FRESH OR THAWED FROZEN CRANBERRIES

¾ CUP [150 G] PACKED LIGHT BROWN SUGAR

1 TBSP RED WINE VINEGAR

4 CUPS [960 ML] CRUSHED CANNED TOMATOES

KOSHER SALT AND FRESHLY GROUND BLACK PEPPER

1 LB [455 G] GROUND BEEF

1 EGG

2 LARGE ONIONS, 1 GRATED ON THE LARGE HOLES OF A BOX GRATER AND 1 THINLY SLICED

continued

**1 MEDIUM CARROT, PEELED AND GRATED
ON THE LARGE HOLES OF A BOX GRATER
VEGETABLE OIL FOR GREASING THE PAN**

1. Fill a large pot halfway with water, set over high heat, and bring to a boil. Use a sharp knife to cut out the cabbage's core, as deep as you can go. When the water is boiling, carefully drop in the head of cabbage, core-side down, and cover the pot tightly with a lid. Boil the cabbage for 10 minutes, then carefully transfer it to a cutting board. Using a pair of tongs, carefully detach as many outer leaves as possible. When you cannot easily remove more leaves, return the cabbage to the water and boil for 10 minutes more. Repeat the process until you have 18 soft, pliable cabbage leaves. Use a sharp knife to trim off the bottom of each cabbage leaf's tough, inner rib (the leaves should roll easily) and set aside.

2. Meanwhile, fill a medium saucepan halfway with water and set over high heat. When the water is boiling, turn the heat to medium, stir in the rice, and cook for 15 minutes; drain and set aside. (The rice should be about halfway cooked.)

continued

3. In another medium saucepan, stir together the cranberries, brown sugar, and vinegar and set over medium heat. Bring the mixture to a simmer and cook, stirring occasionally and mashing the cranberries with a potato masher or the back of a spoon, until the fruit is soft and has released its juice, 3 to 5 minutes. Stir in the tomatoes and 1 tsp of salt. Allow the mixture to come to a boil, then remove from heat. Taste and add more salt, if desired.

4. Add the ground beef, rice, egg, grated onion, carrot, 1 tsp of salt, and a generous amount of pepper to a large bowl. Use your hands to combine the mixture.

5. Preheat the oven to 350°F [180°C]. Lightly grease the bottom of a large Dutch oven or deep 9-by-13-in [23-by-33-cm] baking dish with vegetable oil and arrange the sliced onion rings evenly across the bottom.

6. Form the cabbage rolls: Spoon 2 heaping Tbsp of the meat filling along the bottom edge of a cabbage leaf, leaving about 1/2 in [12 mm] of space. Fold that 1/2 in [12 mm] up over the filling, then fold each side of the leaf toward the center. Roll the cabbage leaf up and away from you, tucking the filling inside a neat package. Place the cabbage roll, seam-side down, into the Dutch oven or baking dish. Repeat with the remaining leaves and filling.

7. Use a ladle to spoon most of the cranberry-tomato sauce over the rolls, reserving about 1 cup [240 ml]. Cover with a tight-fitting lid (or two layers of aluminum foil, if using a baking dish) and bake until the cabbage is tender and the rice is fully cooked, about 60 minutes. Uncover and spoon the reserved sauce over the cabbage rolls. Cover again and bake for 30 minutes longer. Remove from the oven and let rest for 10 to 15 minutes before serving. Serve hot. Store leftovers, covered, in the fridge for up to 3 days.

Balsamic and Brown Sugar Brisket

SERVES 8

Braised brisket began as poverty cuisine—a method of low-and-slow cooking that was capable of transforming a cheap, tough cut of meat into something desirable. Over time, it has become one of the most iconic dishes of the Jewish American kitchen. It is a favorite for the festive meals on Rosh Hashanah, Sukkot, and Passover, and often served as a substantial main alongside potato latkes on Hanukkah. There are countless variations on the theme of brisket, ranging from sweet and tangy to savory and herby.

This version adds brown sugar and balsamic vinegar to the braising liquid, resulting in deep flavor and caramelized edges. Like many braised meat dishes, brisket's flavor improves with time, so plan to make it a day or two before serving. To slice, find the grain (the thin lines that run in one direction along the brisket) and use a sharp knife to thinly slice perpendicular to those lines.

4 TO 5 LB [1.8 KG TO 2.3 KG] BRISKET

KOSHER SALT AND FRESHLY GROUND BLACK PEPPER

3 TBSP VEGETABLE OIL

**3 LARGE RED ONIONS,
HALVED THROUGH THE ROOT AND THINLY SLICED**

8 GARLIC CLOVES, THINLY SLICED

2 BAY LEAVES

1½ CUPS [360 ML] BEEF OR CHICKEN STOCK

⅓ CUP [80 ML] BALSAMIC VINEGAR

1 TBSP RED WINE VINEGAR

continued

⅓ CUP [65 G] PACKED LIGHT BROWN SUGAR
2 TSP ONION POWDER
1 TSP GARLIC POWDER

1. Preheat the oven to 325°F [165°C] and season both sides of the brisket with salt and pepper.

2. Heat 2 Tbsp of the oil in a Dutch oven or large sauté pan set over medium-high heat. Add the brisket and cook, turning once, until browned on both sides, 8 to 10 minutes total. If the brisket does not fit all at once, cut it in half and sear it in batches.

3. Remove the seared brisket from the pot and set aside. Add the remaining 1 Tbsp of oil followed by the onions, garlic, and bay leaves to the pot and cook, stirring often, until the onions soften and the mixture is fragrant, 5 to 10 minutes.

4. Meanwhile, whisk together the stock, balsamic vinegar, red wine vinegar, brown sugar, onion powder, garlic powder, and 1 tsp salt in a medium bowl until fully combined. Transfer the onion mixture to the bottom of a large roasting pan and layer the seared brisket on top. Pour the balsamic mixture over the top, cover tightly with aluminum foil, and transfer to the oven.

5. Cook the meat for 2 hours. Remove from the oven, uncover, and carefully flip the meat to the other side. Re-cover and continue cooking until the meat is fork-tender, 2 to 2^{1}/$_{2}$ hours more.

6. Remove from the oven and transfer the meat to a cutting board; drape loosely with aluminum foil and let rest for 10 to 15 minutes before slicing against the grain. Remove and discard the bay leaves. Use a slotted spoon to remove the onions and arrange around the brisket. Spoon your desired amount of pan juices over the brisket before serving. Serve hot. Store leftovers, covered, in the fridge, for up to 4 days. To reheat, transfer the brisket and any juices to a baking dish and heat in a 325°F [165°C] oven until warmed through, 15 to 20 minutes.

WINE PAIRING
FOR THE HOLIDAYS

At its essence, wine pairing is simple: find a wine you like to drink and serve it. But putting a bit of thought into finding wines that will highlight and complement the food on the table can truly elevate a holiday, or any other special-occasion meal. Here are a few basic guidelines.

Serve richly flavored, dry reds with substantial, hearty dishes like Balsamic and Brown Sugar Brisket (page 99), T'fina Pakaila (page 89), or Mushroom Moussaka (page 37). Nicely chilled, crisp, and fruit-forward white wines pair well with lighter dishes like Roasted Salmon with Lemon-Dill Sauce (page 51), and Kousa b'Jibn (Crustless Zucchini Quiche) (page 19). Rosé, meanwhile, complements just about everything, but is particularly delicious sipped alongside thinly sliced Fennel and Mustard Seed Gravlax (page 49) or Hortopita (Wild Greens Pie) (page 31). On Hanukkah, when fried foods are at the forefront, it's all about the bubbles. Serve chilled prosecco or Champagne to cut through the deep-fried crunch of Pollo Fritto per Hanukkah (page 83) and latkes. Or mix Champagne with orange juice or peach nectar for a quick cocktail that perfectly accompanies a sweet Blintz Soufflé (page 23).

For kosher keepers, wine options were once limited to a handful of syrupy sweet wines that fulfilled the ritual obligation, but weren't terribly exciting to drink. In recent years, a growing number of wine companies in Israel, America, Spain, France, Argentina, New Zealand, and beyond have upped the game, producing high-quality wines that transcend their kosher label. Ask your wine merchant for their recommendations and to keep you up to date with new options.

Lamb Biryani

SERVES 6 TO 8

The mixed rice dishes known as biryani likely have Persian roots, but are most closely associated with Indian cuisine. Perfumed with a complex array of spices, layered with saucy stew (either meat or vegetable), and brightly tinted with saffron, they are fit for a celebration. Biryani is also time-consuming to prepare, which makes it a perfect fit for a special holiday dinner. Indian Jews typically serve lamb biryani for Rosh Hashanah and Sukkot, when warming, festive dishes are de rigueur. When prepping the dish, measure all the spices before cooking, being careful to reserve some turmeric, so they can be added all at once. The Indian spice mix garam masala is available online and at specialty food markets.

½ CUP [120 ML] VEGETABLE OIL

2 LARGE ONIONS, FINELY CHOPPED

KOSHER SALT

1½ TBSP GARAM MASALA

½ TSP RED PEPPER FLAKES

1½ TSP GROUND TURMERIC, DIVIDED

1 TSP GROUND CUMIN

½ TSP FRESHLY GROUND BLACK PEPPER

½ TSP GROUND CARDAMOM

2 CINNAMON STICKS

8 GARLIC CLOVES, FINELY CHOPPED

ONE 2-IN [5-CM] PIECE FRESH GINGER, PEELED AND FINELY CHOPPED

ONE 15-OZ [430-G] CAN DICED TOMATOES

2 LB [910 G] LAMB SHOULDER, CUT INTO 2-IN [5-CM] PIECES

continued

**¼ CUP [10 G] FINELY CHOPPED FRESH CILANTRO,
PLUS MORE FOR SERVING**

½ TSP SAFFRON THREADS, CRUSHED

½ CUP [120 ML] BOILING WATER

**2½ CUPS [500 G] WHITE BASMATI RICE,
SOAKED FOR 30 MINUTES, RINSED, AND DRAINED**

2 BAY LEAVES

1. Heat ¼ cup [60 ml] of the oil in a large sauté pan set over medium-high heat. Add the onions and a generous pinch of salt and cook, stirring occasionally, until softened and lightly browned, 15 to 20 minutes. Transfer the onions to a bowl.

2. Heat the remaining ¼ cup [60 ml] oil in a large Dutch oven or other large saucepan set over medium-high heat. Add the garam masala, red pepper flakes, 1 tsp of the turmeric, the cumin, black pepper, cardamom, and cinnamon sticks and cook, stirring, until sizzling and fragrant, about 30 seconds. Add the garlic, ginger, and tomatoes with their juice and cook, stirring, for 2 to 3 minutes. Add the lamb, season with 1 tsp salt, and cook, stirring occasionally, until the meat is lightly browned, about 5 minutes. Add ¼ cup [60 ml] cool water, cover the pan, turn the heat to medium-low, and cook, stirring occasionally, until the lamb is tender, about 1 hour. Remove from the heat, stir in the browned onions and cilantro. Taste and add more salt, if desired, and set aside.

3. Place the saffron in a small bowl and cover with the boiling water. Stir and set aside. Bring 4 cups [960 ml] of water and 1 tsp salt to a boil in a large saucepan. Add the rice, bay leaves, and remaining 1/2 tsp turmeric. Turn the heat to medium and cook, stirring occasionally, until the rice is halfway cooked, 5 to 10 minutes; drain and set aside.

4. Transfer half of the lamb mixture to the bottom of the saucepan you cooked the rice in. Top the lamb with half of the rice and half of the saffron mixture. Top with the remaining lamb and remaining rice, followed by the remaining saffron. Set the saucepan over low heat, cover, and cook until the rice is fully tender, about 10 minutes. Remove from the heat and let stand, covered, for 10 minutes. Remove the cinnamon sticks and bay leaves and serve hot, sprinkled with fresh cilantro. Store leftovers, covered, in the fridge for up to 3 days.

Mrouzia (Lamb and Dried Fruit Tagine)

SERVES 6

This sweet and savory tagine is enjoyed throughout North Africa, and is traditionally eaten during the Muslim festival Eid al-Adha. North African Jews, meanwhile, serve it on Rosh Hashanah, when the sweetness from the honey and dried fruit is particularly symbolic. Mrouzia is flavored with ras el hanout, a mosaic blend of spices—typically ginger, cinnamon, cumin, coriander, mace, nutmeg, turmeric, and cardamom, among others—that North African cooks use to perfume their cooking. (It can be found in specialty food shops and online.) Some store-bought ras el hanout blends contain salt and some do not, which makes a difference in the final taste of the dish. Taste the blend to see how salty it is and adjust salt levels in the dish accordingly. Serve the mrouzia over steamed couscous.

1½ TBSP RAS EL HANOUT

1 TSP GROUND CINNAMON

1 TSP GROUND GINGER

1 TSP KOSHER SALT, OR MORE AS NEEDED

½ TSP FRESHLY GROUND BLACK PEPPER

¼ TSP RED PEPPER FLAKES

¼ TSP SAFFRON THREADS, CRUSHED

2½ LB [1.2 KG] LAMB SHOULDER, CUT INTO 1-IN [2.5-CM] PIECES

¼ CUP [60 ML] EXTRA-VIRGIN OLIVE OIL

2 MEDIUM ONIONS, HALVED THROUGH THE ROOT AND THINLY SLICED

4 GARLIC CLOVES, THINLY SLICED

1 TBSP TOMATO PASTE

4 CUPS [960 ML] CHICKEN STOCK

continued

2 MEDIUM CARROTS, PEELED, HALVED LENGTHWISE, AND CUT INTO ½-IN [12-MM] SLICES

1 CUP [160 G] PITTED PRUNES, CHOPPED

1 CUP [180 G] DRIED APRICOTS, CHOPPED

1 CUP [120 G] SLICED ALMONDS

¼ CUP [85 G] MILD HONEY

CHOPPED FRESH FLAT-LEAF PARSLEY FOR SERVING

1. Combine the ras el hanout, cinnamon, ginger, salt, black pepper, red pepper flakes, and saffron in a large bowl. Stir in 1/4 cup [60 ml] water to make a paste. Add the lamb pieces and stir well to coat. Cover the bowl and refrigerate overnight.

2. Heat the oil in a large Dutch oven or other heavy saucepan with a lid set over medium heat. Add the onions and garlic and cook, stirring occasionally, until the onions soften, 6 to 8 minutes. Stir in the tomato paste, then add the marinated lamb and chicken stock. Turn the heat to medium-high and bring to a boil, then turn the heat to medium-low, cover, and cook, stirring occasionally, until the meat is tender, about 1 hour.

3. Add the carrots, prunes, apricots, 1/2 cup [60 g] of the almonds, and the honey and continue cooking, covered and stirring often, until the vegetables are tender, about 30 minutes. Uncover and cook until the liquid has thickened slightly, 10 to 15 minutes. Taste and add more salt, if desired.

4. Transfer to a serving dish and serve hot, sprinkled with parsley and the remaining almonds. Store leftovers, covered, in the fridge for up to 3 days.

THE JEWISH HOLIDAYS:
A PRIMER + MEAL IDEAS

The Jewish calendar is filled with festive and contemplative holidays, with Shabbat arriving every week and a major holiday falling nearly every month of the year. The following list is not exhaustive, but covers the holidays where communal meals are typically shared.

SHABBAT

Every week:
Friday at sunset through Saturday at sundown

Shabbat (also known as the Sabbath) commemorates the seventh day of biblical creation, when the Torah says that God stopped to rest and appreciate the world. Observant Jews honor the day by abstaining from driving, using electricity, or engaging in thirty-nine types of broadly defined creative work outlined in the Torah. That time is spent resting, going to synagogue, visiting with friends and family, singing, and, naturally, sharing in three festive meals: Shabbat dinner, Shabbat lunch, and seudah shlishit, a "third meal" held on Saturday afternoon.

MAIN DISHES

Roasted Salmon with Lemon–Dill Sauce, page 51

Chraime (Spicy Sephardi Fish Fillets), page 55

Pesce All'Ebraica (Sweet and Sour Jewish Fish), page 57

Roast Chicken with Leek, Meyer Lemon, and Parsnip, page 75

Chicken Fricassee, page 71

Sofrito (Braised Chicken with Fried Potatoes), page 77

Fesenjan (Persian Chicken, Walnut, and Pomegranate Stew), page 81

T'fina Pakaila (White Bean and Meatball Stew), page 89

Complete the Shabbat table by accompanying these mains with braided challah, a selection of spreads and dips, rice or couscous, and a green salad topped with a bright vinaigrette. Kosher keepers can decide in advance if they plan to have a meat- or dairy-focused meal.

ROSH HASHANAH

Begins the 1st of Tishrei/September or October

Rosh Hashanah is the spiritual head of the Jewish year and the beginning of the festival season known as the High Holidays. It is colloquially known as the Jewish New Year and is seen as a period of contemplation and deep connection. It is also a time of great joy, when family and friends gather together and wish one another a sweet and full year ahead. Rosh Hashanah has many symbolic and seasonal foods associated with it including apples dipped in honey and pomegranates. Some Sephardi communities also hold Rosh Hashanah "seders" at their holiday tables, eating pumpkins, beets, fish heads, dates, black-eyed peas, and other foods that hold symbolic meaning.

MAIN DISHES

Seven-Vegetable Tagine, page 41

Loubia (Black-Eyed Pea Stew), page 45

Chraime (Spicy Sephardi Fish Fillets), page 55

Pesce All'Ebraica (Sweet and Sour Jewish Fish),
page 57

Chicken with Quince and Almonds, page 67

Chicken Fricassee, page 71

Roast Chicken with Leek, Meyer Lemon,
and Parsnip, page 75

Fesenjan (Persian Chicken, Walnut,
and Pomegranate Stew), page 81

T'fina Pakaila (White Bean and Meatball Stew),
page 89

Balsamic and Brown Sugar Brisket, page 99

Lamb Biryani, page 105

Mrouzia (Lamb and Dried Fruit Tagine), page 109

Round out a Rosh Hashanah meal by pairing these
dishes with a round challah, steamed or roasted
vegetables, and rice or couscous.

YOM KIPPUR

Begins the 10th of Tishrei/September or October

Known as the Jewish Day of Atonement, Yom Kippur is a solemn holiday where Jews ask God and one another for forgiveness for any wrongdoings from the past year. Traditionally, people refrain from eating and drinking throughout the twenty-five-hour holiday as a way of directing their energies toward spiritual rather than physical matters. Still, food plays an important role. Before the fast begins, an ample meal is served. And at nightfall after the holiday, people gather for festive break-fast meals, which focus on light, tasty dishes that revive the body after its daylong fast.

MAIN DISHES

Kousa b'Jibn (Crustless Zucchini Quiche), page 19

Blintz Soufflé, page 23

Fennel and Mustard Seed Gravlax, page 49

Pesce All'Ebraica (Sweet and Sour Jewish Fish), page 57

Complete the Yom Kippur break–fast meal with a selection of fresh bagels and/or pita, cream cheese or other spreads, and a seasonal fruit salad.

SUKKOT

Sukkot commemorates the forty years the Israelites spent wandering the desert after their Exodus
from slavery in ancient Egypt. It also celebrates the
season's harvest and bounty. Many families build a
sukkah for the holiday—a temporary outdoor dwelling
made of natural materials and covered with a loose
thatch of tree branches or bamboo that allows those
inside to see the sky. They also acquire a lulav and
etrog—a bundle of myrtle, date, and willow fronds
and a lemony citron, respectively—to wave in the
sukkah as a symbol of Jews' connection to God and
the land. Throughout the weeklong holiday, meals
are enjoyed alfresco in the sukkah, and some people
even sleep inside. Stuffed foods that showcase
seasonal abundance and warming, one-pot dishes
tend to reign on the Sukkot table.

MAIN DISHES

Mushroom Moussaka, page 37

Sofrito (Braised Chicken with Fried Potatoes), page 77

T'fina Pakaila (White Bean and Meatball Stew), page 89

Holishkes (Stuffed Cabbage), page 93

Balsamic and Brown Sugar Brisket, page 99

Lamb Biryani, page 105

Warming sides like roasted root vegetables, simple soups, and rice or bulgur pilaf help round out a Sukkot meal. Kosher keepers can decide in advance if they plan to have a meat- or dairy-focused meal.

HANUKKAH

Begins the 25th of Kislev/Usually December

Called the Holiday of Lights, Hanukkah commemorates the rededication of the Temple in Jerusalem after the Maccabees (a small Judean army) recaptured it from the ancient Greeks. According to the story, the Maccabees were able to find only enough oil to light the Temple's menorah for one night—but it miraculously lasted for eight. In celebration of that miracle of oil, people light menorahs in their homes throughout the eight-night holiday. On the table, deep-fried dishes from potato latkes and fried chicken to doughnuts get their moment in the spotlight.

MAIN DISHES

Eggplant Kuku (Persian Frittata), page 17

**Pollo Fritto per Hanukkah
(Fried Chicken for Hanukkah), page 83**

Balsamic and Brown Sugar Brisket, page 99

Create a cross-cultural Hanukkah table by pairing these dishes with crispy latkes, pickled veggies, and fried doughnuts for dessert.

Note: Kosher keepers who want to serve the kuku alongside meat can omit the feta.

PURIM

Begins the 14th of Adar/February or March

Purim is, without a doubt, one of the most festive holidays on the Jewish calendar. It celebrates the heroism of Queen Esther, a Jewish woman who became queen of Persia and saved her people from destruction at the hands of her king-husband's wicked advisor, Haman. People celebrate by listening to the megillah (scroll) of Esther's story read aloud, and by dressing up in costume and throwing raucous, boozy parties. Desserts such as hamantaschen are the most widely recognized Purim treats. But many families also host a traditional meal called a seudah on Purim day, which features its own culinary delights.

MAIN DISHES

Eggplant Kuku (Persian Frittata), page 17

Berkuks (Sweet Couscous with Milk), page 27

Poppy Seed Schnitzel, page 87

Highlight the Purim seudah table with a wide selection of dips, salads, and spreads, and lots of challah or pita for dipping. End the meal with hamantaschen, marzipan, and other festive sweets. Kosher keepers can decide in advance if they plan to have a meat- or dairy-focused meal.

PASSOVER

Begins the 15th of Nisan/March or April

Passover celebrates the Israelites' Exodus from ancient Egypt and their movement from a life of slavery to one of freedom. Traditionally, Jews abstain from eating chametz (leavened foods made from wheat, barley, oats, rye, and spelt) throughout the weeklong holiday. More strictly observant Jews from an Ashkenazi background also abstain from corn, millet, rice, legumes, and other foods, collectively called *kitniyot*, which could be mistaken for chametz. Instead, Jews turn to matzo, a specially made unleavened bread eaten throughout Passover. Families and friends gather together on the first night (and for many families, the first two nights) of Passover for the seder—a retelling of the Passover story that includes many symbolic foods, four cups of wine, and a sumptuous feast right in the middle.

MAIN DISHES

Mina (Matzo Pie with Leeks and Spinach), page 35

Chraime (Spicy Sephardi Fish Fillets), page 55

Chicken Fricassee, page 71

Roast Chicken with Leek, Meyer Lemon, and Parsnip, page 75

Balsamic and Brown Sugar Brisket, page 99

Springlike, Passover-friendly sides like roasted asparagus, new potatoes in herby vinaigrette, and bright salads brimming with snappy cucumber and creamy avocado help transform these main dishes into a seder meal. Kosher keepers can decide in advance if they plan to have a meat- or dairy-focused meal.

SHAVUOT

Begins the 6th of Sivan/May or June

Falling seven weeks after Passover, Shavuot
commemorates the story of when God revealed the
Torah to the Israelites at Mount Sinai. Agriculturally
speaking, it also marks the end of the barley harvest
in ancient Israel and the beginning of the wheat
harvest. People tend to stay up all night on Shavuot,
studying together to honor the traditions' most
sacred text. Ashkenazi communities also have a
tradition of eating dairy foods such as blintzes
and cheesecake.

MAIN DISHES

Kousa b'Jibn (Crustless Zucchini Quiche), page 19

Blintz Soufflé, page 23

Hortopita (Wild Greens Pie), page 31

Roasted Salmon with Lemon-Dill Sauce, page 51

Bring a dairy-focused Shavuot meal together with a barley or bulgur salad brimming with nuts, dried fruit, and goat cheese, and a chilled soup such as borscht, topped with sour cream.

 ACKNOWLEDGMENTS

So many thank-yous, so little space! Here goes:

Thank you, thank you to my agent, Jenni Ferrari-Adler, for her sage advice and constant support. Thank you to my editors Sarah Billingsley and Deanne Katz, design director Vanessa Dina, marketing and publicity managers Alexandra Brown and Amy Cleary, and the whole team at Chronicle Books. It feels so great to hand over a manuscript and know that it is in good, caring hands.

Yet again, the food styling and photography team completely rocked. Linda Pugliese, Monica Pierini, Paige Hicks, Susan Kim, and Dinah Bess Rotter: thank you for letting me crash the photo shoot, and for bringing the recipes to full-color life.

Thanks to my friends and family for trying out some of the recipes in their home kitchens, and for their helpful feedback. Abi Goodman, Avia Moore, Beth Shulman, Eve Stoller, Gayle Squires, Laurel Kratochvila, Nancy Eson and Lena Eson Roe, Lindsey Paige, Lorin Sklamberg, Miriam Bader, Molly Yeh, Ora Fruchter and Bradford Jordan, Owen Gottlieb and Abby Bellows— you are all generous and amazing.

Many thanks to Ron and Leetal Arazi of New York Shuk, whose delicious harissa pastes are the only ones I use in my kitchen, and who first introduced me to berkuks. My recipe uses store-bought couscous, but I strongly encourage anyone who finds themselves in Brooklyn to take a hand-rolled couscous-making class from Ron and Leetal.

Thank you to my family: Carol Koenig, Rena and Chaim Fruchter, Seth Koenig and Sara Shank, Temim Fruchter, Ora Fruchter and Bradford Jordan, and Dasi Fruchter—your encouragement, ideas, and enthusiasm keep me going!

And finally, thank you to my big and little fellas, Yoshie and Max. Here's to building a home together filled with delicious food, great music, and lots of love and community.

INDEX

Zivar Amrami

Leah Koenig is a writer and cookbook author whose work has appeared in the *New York Times*, the *Wall Street Journal*, *Saveur*, *Epicurious*, *Rachael Ray Every Day*, *Tablet*, and *The Forward*, among other publications. She is the author of three cookbooks, including *Modern Jewish Cooking* (Chronicle, 2015) and *The Little Book of Jewish Appetizers* (Chronicle, 2017). Leah lives in Brooklyn, New York, with her husband and son, and leads cooking demonstrations across the globe. Visit her online at www.leahkoenig.com and on Instagram @leah.koenig.